T0353697

FATHER DO YOU HAVE A MINUTE?

Come unto Me

MILTON WHITE

BALBOA.PRESS
A DIVISION OF HAY HOUSE

Copyright © 2025 Milton White.

All rights reserved. No part of this book may be used or reproduced by any means, graphic, electronic, or mechanical, including photocopying, recording, taping or by any information storage retrieval system without the written permission of the author except in the case of brief quotations embodied in critical articles and reviews.

Balboa Press books may be ordered through booksellers or by contacting:

Balboa Press
A Division of Hay House
1663 Liberty Drive
Bloomington, IN 47403
www.balboapress.com
844-682-1282

Because of the dynamic nature of the Internet, any web addresses or links contained in this book may have changed since publication and may no longer be valid. The views expressed in this work are solely those of the author and do not necessarily reflect the views of the publisher, and the publisher hereby disclaims any responsibility for them.

The author of this book does not dispense medical advice or prescribe the use of any technique as a form of treatment for physical, emotional, or medical problems without the advice of a physician, either directly or indirectly. The intent of the author is only to offer information of a general nature to help you in your quest for emotional and spiritual well-being. In the event you use any of the information in this book for yourself, which is your constitutional right, the author and the publisher assume no responsibility for your actions.

Any people depicted in stock imagery provided by Getty Images are models, and such images are being used for illustrative purposes only. Certain stock imagery © Getty Images.

Print information available on the last page.

ISBN: 979-8-7652-5870-5 (sc)
ISBN: 979-8-7652-5869-9 (e)

Balboa Press rev. date: 01/03/2025

Contents

Dedication

This book is dedicated to the one person who taught me to, stand up and be counted. For I have a voice and I will be heard! They taught me to have sight beyond sight, listen as well as hear, speak, and say what must be said at the right time. She was my teacher, even when I wasn't in a classroom, I was still being taught!!

So I dedicate this book to my beloved deceased sister, Geraldine White. You have ALWAYS been my inspiration for self growth. I love you Dee Dee.

I also dedicate this book to the beautiful Spirit filled Woman of God. Sarah Jacocks, a woman whose kindness and teaching lead me to repent of my sins and receive the Blood Atonement of Jesus the Christ,(Yeshua). She will be greatly missed by her daughters, Diane, ReNee, Wanda and son Raymond and their family tree. Rest my friend always until the Rapture.

Your brother,
Milton

Father Do you Have a Minute

Father do You have a minute?
My Father, I need to talk to you,
Just so much I'm going through.
Without You God, what can I do?
So listen to me for a moment or two?
Feeling down, my bills are pressing,
Raising a family can be.so stressing.
Help me God so I'm not guessing,
lean on You, to receive my blessing.
As times get tough my spirit feel low,
I start to wonder, where can I go?
Help my mustard seed of faith to grow,
Just whisper and say, child, I know!!
I know You're here, for in You I abide,
Your passionate Love, I feel inside.
In Your Shadow, Father, may I hide?
Holy Spirit, I need You, be my guide.
You watch the birds, number my hair,
My burdens, throw them anywhere!!
Lord Jesus, these things I now share,
Father thank You, I know You care.

By Milton White

Will I Ever

It's hard to walk in the narrow path.
been washed in Jesus Blood bath.
Trying not to fall to Satanic crafts,
but run to You with a mad dash.
Times may get tough, that's a given,
not because of the life you're living.
All babies, kids, every men and women,
was Adam and Eve curse for sinning.
Go to church, then later we're fighting,
judging others, our tongues backbiting.
Forgetting who is our Lord of Lighting,
maybe it's time for a JESUS sighting.
None of us is perfect, no not even one,
It's why God sent Jesus, His only Son.
Taking my sins to Jesus Christ I run,
He's the Door, to Him He said, "Come".
Will I ever live my life as I should?
Will I follow my Savior if I could?
Stop doing wrong and try to be good,
Help me my God, to do as You would!!
Will I ever stop my wrongs to do right,
Not in darkness, but follow the Light.
Although I'm blind, You are my sight,
this is Milton, thank You God for life!!!

By Milton White October 2023

Imagine That

Imagine that you suddenly awake,
shallow breathing you slowly make.
What's going on? My body ache,
I can't move, force myself to shake.
Why do my body, refuse to move,
I can't make it get into a groove.
My body control, did I really lose?,
What's wrong with me? I'm confused!!
My body is twisted over to the left,
a human pretzel, describes me best.
My *family*, see's my twisted up mess,
standing with me, loving me no less.
Weeks, months, came healing time,
I strengthed, this sick body of mine.
Prayers, work, a straightened spine,
a MIRACLE awakening, now in line.
I'm moving, walking every single day,
even getting stronger, I've gotta say.
My body, no stroke, will no more play,
It's now a temple now a place to pray.
Imagine that, feeling great within,
no strokes, seizures, I can even bend
Was given up for dead, oh but then,
God heard prayers, of family and friends.

By Milton White July 20th 2023

Forever

Forever Merciful God is who You are,
Healing my many scrapes and scars.
Self-righteous rags You will discard,
Thank You my Bright Morning Star.
Forever Loving God You are to me,
A sinless Lamb who died on a tree,
With that single act You did decree,
With Loving Kindness I draw to thee.
Your Goodness Lord I know is here,
And I strongly feel it everywhere.
To others I try to make it so clear,
On the cross, my sins did Jesus bare.
Forever Lord, is Your Amazing Grace,
We are hidden in Your secret place.
Under Your Wings God, are we safe.
Rest a little, then continue our race.

By Milton White

I Shall Stand

Trials will come, but I shall stand,
I'm no different than any other man.
Trials of life is part of God's plan,
Trust Father God and take His hand.
When I stand it's all because of Christ,
All my strength is from His Sacrifice.
His Blood Sacrifice, gave me new life,
Death the grave and sin, <u>has</u> no bite.
Jesus the Christ, He was beat all night,
In the dark, oh, they tortured the Light.
He was a horrible beaten down sight,
He still held on with all of His might.
On the Cross, clouds dark so gray.
Still 7 teaching He yet had to say.
A malefactor joined in mocking play,
But one,' you'll be in Paradise today".
That's why I stand He did it for me,
Became my curse and died on a tree.
He'll return one day for all to see,
Crucified for my sins, I'll stand for He.

By Milton White

The Fight Part One

There's so many types of fights,
Swinging with hands, left and right.
You work out, both day and night,
Keeping your opponent in your sight!!
Its the same, in our Christian walk,
The way we speak, when we talk.
We have to train hard daily, as we ought,
Battle for Christ, and you won't fall.
My opponent is one we called Satan,
Because we follow Jesus, he's hating.
With temptation, he starts his baiting,
I'm with Jesus, on HIM I'm waiting.
Satan hit me with his blind disease,
And any strokes, took me to my knees.
Sarcoid, my lungs, so hard to breathe,
Four biopsies later, it gave me ease.
After that, life was somewhat better,
then Satan hit me with a double hitter.
Having a stroke, made me so bitter,
Seizures too? Still, I'm NO quitter!!!
Surgeries, on my knees, I count eight,
The last, titanium, left knee replaced.
With appendix removed, came Grace,
Colon Cancer found, it wasn't too late.

Later on, as I went to take a pee,
darkened blood, was all I would see!!
Blood clots in bladder, doctor's seized,
another battle.that was won for me!
I took shots & boosters for Covid-19,
It still hit me hard, like a laser beam!!
This was a nightmare not a dream,
I, hurted so much, I often screamed!!!
Two weeks later, they sent me home,
Satan sent pain through my bones.
Can't he just please leave me alone??
But my God acted from His throne.

Part One by Milton White 5/10/24

All By Myself

I created the Earth and the Heavens,
Hallowed and rested on day seven.
I made man, but then he fell to sin,
Now I must go down, be his champion.
Creation made with the Father's help,
But this Salvation, I have to do Myself.
Man sinful soul must be redeemed,
Only My Blood, can man be cleaned.
All by Myself will I go to the Earth,
Show My Father, I can see their worth.
We put in man a spirit and soul to live,
Born again, a new chance we'll give.
With My Life, I Gracefully lay it down,
Accept My Blood to be Glory bound,
By Myself, you are now redeemed,
By My Blood, now you're cleaned.

By Milton White

More Reason to Love You

I went to Church as a young lad,
can't remember if I was happy or sad.
We had to go because Mom and Dad,
said if we go, we'd make God glad.
For Church they gave us all a dime,
but it didn't go to offering all the time.
What you gonna buy at the store?
I'm buying me candy, for that belly of mine.
The preacher talked, what he'd said,
I can't remember if it went to my head.
I fell asleep hard, like I was dead,
couldn't wait to go home to get in bed.
As I grew older and read HIS book,
my interest took a more serious look.
couldn't put it down, now I'm hooked,
God's Words of love, my heart took.
It's not about money, or my clothes,.
maybe it's all about HIM, I suppose.
HE blessed me from my head to toes,
I'll keep fighting, that's the way it goes,
The doctors, nurses did their best,
straightened up my spine, so I'd rest.
I'm feeling this stroke, less and less,
God's Grace help me, through my test.

Taken to the hospital, family mourned,
even the doctors thought I was gone.
In the fetus position, like I was born,
twisted up body, my dry skin torned.
But so many prayers went up above,
healing Mercy came down like a dove.
Now forever in my life, just because,
I've got a reason to give God my love.

By Milton White. August 2023

Who Am I?

Who am I? I ask you, still very young,
People around, yet I'm so alone.
Who am I? Really, I need to know,
I need a mate to walk the path I go.
Who's Milton? There's times I wonder.
A lonely man, on this I sit and ponder.
God, please, is there a mate for me?
To love just me, before I go to eternity.
Remember, You gave Adam his Eve,
Even had a family, and she conceived!
I'm asking You Father, so let me know.
Will I get a mate, and a family to grow?

By Milton White

Behold the Man

Behold the Man He came from above,
Didn't bring hate, He came with Love.
Through 42 generations came for me,
Sacrificed His life, and died on a tree.
Behold the Man, He taught us to live,
Showing Love, Mercy, to others give.
To those who's less fortunate than us,
Giving from the heart without a fuss.
Behold the Man walking in the garden,
Because of man's sins, find a pardon.
God Son Jesus, took up man's cup,
Full of man's sins, He drank it all up.
Behold that Man, He didn't stay dead,
3 days and nights, spoke in Hell's bed.
He rose up in Glory, His Power Divine,
Redeemed Blood, removed our crime.
Behold the Lamb of God, Jesus Christ,
He came from Glory, to pay sin price.
Behold the Man with Perfect Love,
Soon to be with Him in heaven above.

By Milton White

How Beautiful

Such sinful creatures both you and I,
so Jesus came down from the sky.
He saw beauty in us through His eyes,
To redeem us to God, He had to die.
The Book said in us no good dwells,
We're born in sin, it's in our DNA cells.
We were sinners and destined for hell,
Relax, more good news, the Bible tells.
Look how they just beat him like that!
Whips that tore the skin off his back.
Spiked thorns, they made Him a hat,
This is Love, that's a un-natual fact.
So Beautiful that God truly loves me,
He let them crucify His Son on a tree.
This was done for the world to see,
The price for our sins was paid by HE.

By Milton White
Poem #3

The Fight Part One

Fight's Not Over, Part One

There's so many types of fights,
Swinging with hands, left and right.
You work out, both day and night,
Keeping your opponent in your sight!!
Its the same, in our Christian walk,
The way we speak, when we talk.
We have to train hard daily, as we alt,
Battle for Christ, and you won't fall.
My opponent is one we called Satan,
Because we follow Jesus, he's hating.
With temptation, he starts his baiting,
I'm with Jesus, on HIM I'm waiting.
Satan hit me with his blind disease,
And any strokes, took me to my knees.
Sarcoid, my lungs, so hard to breathe,
Four biopsies later, it gave me ease.
After that, life was somewhat better,
then Satan hit me with a double hitter.
Having a stroke, made me so bitter,
Seizures too? Still, I'm NO quitter!!!
Surgeries, on my knees, I count eight,
The last, titanium, left knee replaced.
With appendix removed, came Grace,
Colon Cancer found, it wasn't too late.

Later on, as I went to take a pee,
darkened blood, was all I would see!!
Blood clots in bladder, doctor's seized,
another battle.that was won for me!
I took shots & boosters for Covid-19,
It still hit me hard, like a laser beam!!
This was a nightmare not a dream,
I, hurted so much, I often screamed!!!
Two weeks later, they sent me home,
Satan sent pain through my bones.
Can't he just please leave me alone??
But my God acted from His throne.

Part One by Milton White 5/10/24

I'm Still Here

I can't believe, how I hurt so much,
from my heads top, down to my butt.
Sometimes I don't even feel my guts,
in my mind, I rarely know what's what.
Why is my body twisted up like this?
I don't even know how, to take a piss.
Where's all the time that I missed??
Do I have family, Kids, or marital bliss?.
Now clouds are slowly going away,
I'm getting better, stronger, day by day.
Even a few words I'm starting to say,
but still rehabbing in my bed I stay.
I recognize family, more and more,
coming to visit me through the door.
Times I can put my feet on the floor,
come on Milt, make your health soar.
Doctors, nurses, cleaners and aides,
earning the money that they made.
Even after "he'll die" everyone said,
GOD gave me a miracle, where I laid.
Family helped when they came there,
looking at what I was, brougt my tears.
Thanking God, family, for all this year,
no longer facing death, I'm still HERE.

By Milton White. August 2023

Why?

Why am I feeling, like such a mess???
God, is this another one of Your test!?
I hope not, I'm not feeling at my best,
Can You just hold me, to Your breast?
I had a stroke, it's a real bad one too,
couldn't remember, what I should do.
A voice said Milton, I wondered, who?,
could this be me, they're speaking to?
Months later, things slowly changed,
I knew then," hey, I'm that man"!!
Still this body was wretched with pain,
"Who am I? Am I going insane".?!!
Several weeks later, my mind returned,
like a caterpillar, to a butterfly, reborn.
Looked at my body, it's so deformed,
how long this mess, been going on?
I got better with this twisted up spine,
I sat up alone, on the bed of mine.
Therapists, nurses, aides, ever so kind,
helped Milton get back on his behind.
With that stroke, I couldn't eat a thing,
soon I ate salads and chicken wings.
Even McDonald's and Burger King,
my throat better, I even tried to sing.
First rode around in my wheelchair,
with my walker, the therapists stared.

"You're much better, but Milt take care"
don't want you to fall, on your rear!!
My arms stronger, time to go home,
They helped me heal, to be strong.
For what y'all did, I praise you in song,
You made me right, removed wrong.
My doctors, nurses, aides, therapists
So long of a helpful and healing list.
I'm not being sexist, so dont be pissed,
I'd like to give you all a loving kiss.
What happened in the months by,
Sometimes I'm happy, times I just cry.
I hunch my shoulders, with a sigh,
Thanks God for life, I won't ask…. why.
Thanks…

Milton White October 2023

Troubled Times

Sometimes when I first wake up,
praised God, my eyes aren't still shut.
No alarm clock or blankets tugged,
but Your Mercy and Love from above.
Many sickness made me feel so less,
Lung disease Sarcoidosis, in my chest.
Strokes, seizures, because of stress,
some of the reasons I'm in this mess.
Retinitis Pigmentosa, disease of eyes
I've asked you God, just tell me why.
Prostate, colon cancer, made me sigh,
I felt in the world, this was goodbye.!!
I've got sleep apnea, low thyroid too,
add a heart aneurysm, what can I do?
Parkinson's, neuropathy, oh, no shoes,
twisted spinal cord, could barely move.
I've been blind àlí of my known years,
thought glasses it would be a cure.
A specialist said, let's see what's here,
eyes of cataracts, removed them there.
Some people said that I'm still hot,
How's that, with all these things I got!!!
4 lung biopsies, prostate almost shot,
Colon cancer, out of the fire, to the pot.

Knee surgeries, 5 on right, 2 on left,
titanium knee on left, wasn't the best.
I did cocaine, never smoked 'cess,
but in 1988, I gave it all a needed rest.
I've fought demons throughout my life,
I've become calm, I don't live in strife.
I've become spiritual with a new high,
I've learned to walk closer with God.

By Milton White October 11th 2023

The Fights Not Over, Part Two

To the E.R. I had to constantly go,
because I developed bladder woes.
When I would pee, blood would flow,
that Satan still refused to let me go!!!
That was September, now December?
Where's time? I just can't remember!!
Why's this tube down in my member?
Who am I, don't even know my gender!
Huh, I've been in a Coma you say???
for a few months, and many of days.
Didn't my family see me this way??
did they even get together to pray?
Kindly tell me why I can't even talk,
my legs feel numb, oh, I begin to walk.
Finally words sounding like the Hulk,
I realize that this is all Satan's fault!!
Awaking now to whom everyone is,
even tried to fill me in, about all of this.
Is this my wife, who gave me a kiss??
How'd my body take a horrible twist?
Weeks later, they sat me up in bed,
I had a twisted neck and hurting head.
Many thought that soon I'd be dead,
have faith in GOD, is what I was fed!!

Mental battles were just as tough,
I fought with nurses, yelled and cuss
Times I felt, like my head would bust,
Come on Milt, in GOD is your trust!!!
I've been down, but again, Milt's up,
can't let this stroke, drag me to dust.
Make your body, put up a strong fuss,
believe in GOD above and not in luck.
Months later, NOW, Milt look at you!!!
GOD proved His Words are so True.
In a corner, family's not sad or blue,
Agreed in praying, it bought me thru.
Look at me now, I'm walking around,
I'm talking a lot, singing loving sounds.
Last year many put me in the ground,
Now look, A king with a healing crown!
Thanks to all, who prayed continually,
God's eyes are open, and He saw me.
I'm not as healthy, not, as I used to be,
I'm alive, sweet Jesus, I thank Thee.

By Milton White January 2024

Wonderfully Made

You created Heavens and the stars,
The Sun, Earth, Venus and Mars.
Your Majesty expands near and far,
Oh Alpha, Omega, Bright Morning Star.
A little lower than Angels I'm made,
In Your image is what You said.
You're here to guide us to be our aid,
Thanks Father, I'm Wonderfully made!
Perfectly created, yet we fell in sin,
That must have hurt You deep within.
Jesus crucified, a new day to begin,
Soon to live in Heaven with Him.
With Your Salvation what joy we feel,
Even with our faults, You love us still.
For Salvation, You presented no bill,
You said, Worship God, obey His Will.
You made things lovely to our eyes,
Yet real beauty, is Christ in our lives.
The Lamb of God for us was crucified,
Wonderful Salvation for you and I.

.......By Milton White
...Poem #3

Eyes Have Not Seen

My eyes have never seen Your Glory,
Even after I read Your Loving Story.
God created a spirit, soul, and features,
And how Jesus died for us creatures.
It still hasn't registered into my heart,
Of being born again, gives me a new start.
Or how His Blood made me so clean,
How His Sacrifice, I'm now redeemed!!
I'm trying to take in His Divine Word,
So my spirit can accept all I heard.
Let the Fruits of the Spirit grow in me,
So God's Light, shine ever brightly.
Tell me how will this body survive?
If it's changed in a twinkling of an eye!
Our reward is with Him I'm told,
Have a mansion, walk a Street of Gold.
There's no way can I ever understand,
God rewards for His born again man.
A Golden crown and a white robe?
Still the greatest story ever told!

By Milton White

I Will Cry No More

One day there'll come a time,
When I will shed no more tears.
Sadness won't even come to mind,
Of all the pain throughout my years.
I have cried when I feel so alone,
And I really don't like feeling that way.
Complaining and pouting with a moan,
Wishing for the end of my crappy day.
So tell me why do I act crazy like this?
I even know what I'm doing is wrong.
If I don't get my way, I only get pissed,
Why don't I just Praise God in a song?
Trust me there will come a Holy day,
No more will my personal tears flow.
I just know Jesus the Christ will say,
There's no crying in heaven, oh no.
Take a look, there's no watery eyes,
That was left behind in your past life.
It was all finished when Jesus died,
That Lamb of God was our Sacrifice.
Jesus came down, He lived for me,
Then was crucified for one such as I?
He Resurrected for all to see,
Son of God, forever I will thank Thee.

By Milton White

Lead Me

Lead me to the Rock higher than I,
That secret place where I can abide,
in my Father's love I'm safe inside,
His words in my heart I forever hide.
Lead me to that Old Rugged Cross,
A lesson of love Jesus Himself taught.
Hanging on a tree my soul He bought,
Shedding His Blood He said "no cost"!
Lead me to His Bleeding Pierced side,
Beaten and bruised for us, you and I.
Finally, "My God, My God" He cried,
"It is finished", laid His head down, He died!
Lead me to Jesus, my Precious Lord,
His Blood washed, all the sins I bore.
Jesus rose in Power, forever more,
Jesus, your Bride we sweetly adore!!

By Milton White

Enter

With Thanksgivings I enter Thy gates,
I Worship You God in this Holy place.
I'm surrounded by Your loving Grace,
Almost like I see You, face to Face.
I enter in Thy Holy courts with Praise,
For You're Mercies through this day.
Upon Your Glory one day I'll gaze,
Your Holy Blood approved my case.
May I enter into Your Holy of Holies?
Your Word said I can come in boldly!!
To you Christ Jesus I surrender totally,
Mind, heart, soul, I surrender wholly.
Into my heart Jesus please enter in,
I believe in You make me born again.
Your Blood has washed away my sins,
Father, the Son, me, now we're all kin!!

By Milton White

The One

Who do I turn to when I have a need,
Keeping me safe from harm and fear.
Who with His Spirit will gently lead,
to His pasture to keep me safe there.
Who's the One who won't stop caring?
Even there when you're full of doubt.
His loving Mercy He's always sharing,
And His Grace, He always pours out.
Who's the One who fights my wars?
No battle He has never, ever lost!!
Killed, buried, arose, alive evermore,
Jesus, the One, Himself paid the cost.
He's the One Who'll returned one day,
In His presence forever we'll stay,
Jesus the Christ, He's the One.
Jesus is the Way, the Truth, the Life,
He's also, "I AM, THAT I AM"!!!
He is the Lamb Who was Sacrificed,
Now we have life never to be damned.
His Church, His Bride, He'll say, Come.
Who loves my soul? Jesus God's Son.
Who's my All In all? Jesus the One,
I love You Jesus, You're the ONE!!!

By Milton White

Pardon me Lord

Pardon me Lord for I have sinned,
I need Your forgiveness right now.
Let the cleansing of my soul begin,
So I too one day will wear a crown.
Mercy Lord, overlook my weakness,
I walked In the flesh one more time.
Humble me with a Spirit of meekness,
So it's Power will keep me in line.
Help me God to love my neighbor,
To love them as I would myself.
You love me my Sweet Savior,
Who am I not to love someone else?
Part of Me Lord for being so bold,
Many material things you gave me.
Did I share enough? Was I too cold?,
Closed my eyes so I wouldn't see!!
Help me show mercy like You Father,
Extending all kindness to others,
So loving humanity won't be a bother,
Showing light to sisters and brothers.

By Milton White

No Weapon Formed

No weapon formed can ever hurt *me*,
God is with me always this you'll see.
I'm not a butterfly, *nor a bumblebee,*
just a branch on Father God's Tree.
There will be strong terrible storms,
Hang in there Milt, you're in God's hand,
a spiritual battle, I don't understand.
I've got to try, to do all that I can,
spreading His Word in this land.
I'm going to be hit and knocked down,
Very little smiles, too many frowns.
I'll pray making soft weeping sounds,
ask God for strength to get around.
Satan, the enemy will try everything,
dont want us to praise Jesus our King!
Devils and demons, their evil bring,
but Jesus Blood, will clip their wings!!
Being angry, they pull out all the stops,
demons want to lift Satan up on top.
But God's Angels, His Heavenly Cops,
arrest them to stop them on the spot.
Now with faith, we wear God's Armor,
Heaven says trust, the world, is Karma.
Seeds of hope, the Gospel Farmers,
a life in Christ, so sin can't harm them.

God help me to lift the shield of Faith,
Give me the victory to Heaven's Gate.
He provided a table, gave me a plate,
of Salvation, and His Amazing Grace.

By Milton White September 24th 2024

One More

One more battle I must survive,
Again I'll show God's victory cry.
Battered and bruised yet still alive,
I can't lose with Christ at my side.
One more tear do I have to cry,
I'll fight the good fight, as it's said.
I have the strength since Jesus bled,
I won't let weakness go to my head,
God's Loving Kindness I've been fed.
One more trial I must go through,
So give me faith, as I believe in You.
I know exactly what I have to do,
Rely on Him who's Faithful and True.
One more sinner, I'll tell about Christ,
His Sacrificed Blood, is Eternal Life.
Forget darkness come to God's Light,
A blind sinner, now has Christ's sight.

By Milton White

Independence Day

We wave our flags on this holiday,
"God bless America", we proudly say.
Blood was spilled on this land's clay,
fighting for freedom was the only way.
Lives were lost, still America believed,
Until the last man falls, don't be deceived.
Our bloody flag, our beacon of peace,
until our salvation, finally is achieved.
The Father sent Jesus into this world,
to save men, women, boys, and girls.
to Heaven's Gates of gold and pearls,
where we'll get, our precious reward.
Our flag is stained with Jesus Blood,
to free us, Christ came from up above.
Washed our sins, the Cross, His tub,
Independence Day, by Jesus Love!!!

By Milton White July 6th 2023

* Qgaa,@And à

Man of Power, Man of Love

You raise Me up with Your right arm,
Keeping me from all types of harm.
Your Holy Blood is stronger than sin,
It enabled me to be boring again!
Your name mentioned, demons flee,
They know Your power lives in me.
Thinking yeah, He died on the cross,
Oh, He arose, showed them He's Boss!
His love for us kept Him nailed there,
Crucified shows how much He cared.
"Save Yourself" malefactors yelled,
He stayed so we wouldn't go to hell.
He started making us a new home,
Even a gold crown for my dome.
He's coming in a twinkling of an eye,
Because we broke free of Satan's lies.
Now I'm doing right and not wrong,
That Man of Power, Love is so strong.
I Glorify God with the life I now live,
To others His love I want to give.
He's a Man of Power, a Man of Love,
Mary's baby, is our Savior from above.
That Lamb of God, a bloody mess,
He saved my soul, now I'm blessed.

By Milton White

Put Thou My Tears

Into a bottle, put Thou my tears,
I've gathered many, through the years.
I come unto You because You care,
Where else can I go? Lord, where?
Put Thou my tears into Thy jar,
Soothe away my hurts and scars.
Many situations was ever so hard,
You're the Light, take me from dark.
Please wipe these tears off my face,
These trials Lord, I don't want to taste.
Hurl them away, maybe outer space?
A Sea of Forgetting, is a better place.
Help me Lord, my life's such a mess,
Hold Me Lord Jesus to Your breast.
O' Shepherd lead me through my test,
At Your altar Lord God I kneel to rest.
Put Thou my life into Thy Holy hands,
Hold me up Lord and help me stand.
I'll sing and shout, in a praise dance,
No more tears, in Your heavenly land.

By Milton White

Printed in the United States
by Baker & Taylor Publisher Services

Printed in the United States
by Baker & Taylor Publisher Services